THE YALE DRAMA SERIES

David Charles Horn Foundation

The Yale Drama Series is funded by the generous support of the David Charles Horn Foundation, established in 2003 by Francine Horn to honor the memory of her husband, David. In keeping with David Horn's lifetime commitment to the written word, the David Charles Horn Foundation commemorates his aspirations and achievements by supporting new initiatives in the literary and dramatic arts.

Utility

EMILY SCHWEND

Foreword by Nicholas Wright

Yale UNIVERSITY PRESS NEW HAVEN & LONDON

Yale University Press books may be purchased in quantity for educational, business, or promotional use. For information, please e-mail sales.press@yale .edu (U.S. office) or sales@yaleup.co.uk (U.K. office).

Set in Galliard type by Integrated Publishing Solutions.
Printed in the United States of America.

ISBN 978-0-300-22442-9 (paperback : alk. paper)
Library of Congress Control Number: 2017933039
A catalogue record for this book is available from the British Library.

This paper meets the requirements of ANSI/NISO Z39.48-1992 (Permanence of Paper).

10 9 8 7 6 5 4 3 2 1

All inquiries regarding this play for performance (in whole or in part) or otherwise should be addressed to Leah Hamos at the Gersh Agency, 41 Madison Avenue, 33rd Floor, New York, N.Y. 10010, attn.: Leah Hamos; lhamos@gersh.com.

Contents

Foreword

Years ago, when we were both working at the Royal Court Theatre in London, a friend asked me who I thought most kept the art of theatre alive. I don't remember what my answer was, but hers was actors. Everyone else, she went on to say, follows fashion. Playwrights, directors, and designers change their subjects, their styles, and even their convictions in order not to appear out of date. Actors don't. They never try to be more abstract, more expressionist, or more topical. Year after year, decade after decade, they keep faith with the essential factor of their art: realism.

One can see a problem with this argument: get on to YouTube and you'll see any number of once acclaimed stage actors of the past looking very unconvincing indeed. (Though the best film actors—Cary Grant, Katharine Hepburn, Anna Magnani, Anton Walbrook—look as good today as they ever did.) But my friend's notion of realism as the central resource of theatre has stuck with me ever since and I think it's true.

Realism is a capacious, malleable form. It can be bold and extravagant. It's far from being a photographic copy of life: it happily accommodates song, verse, fancy, and illogic. It revels in wordless metaphor: think of the glorious last act of *Three Sisters* in which the story is told almost entirely in sound . . . a departing band, a gunshot . . . and images: a fork on a chair, a false beard, a woman looking out of a window. Its hallmark is that it tells the truth about people: not so much what we are like (though that too) but what we are like with each other.

I say all this by way of introduction to a play that is both realistic and remarkable. It was picked as the winner of the Yale Drama Series competition by a panel including me and twelve others: playwrights Alice Birch, Howard Brenton, Rebecca Lenkiewicz, and Barney Norris; directors Natalie Abrahami, Jeff James, and Amelia Sears; dramaturgs Jack Bradley (formerly with the National Theatre), Tom Lyons (National Theatre), and David Tushingham (Dramaturg Salzburg Festival); Peter Ansorge, former commissioning editor for Channel Four, and Dinah Wood, editorial director for drama at Faber and Faber.

Among us, we assessed around sixteen hundred plays. They had been submitted anonymously, so we had no way of knowing whether the playwrights were male, female, or optional, or what their background, experience, or heritage might be.

Having divided them up between us, we gathered around my kitchen table for two meetings. At the first of these, we described whichever plays we'd read that we thought were possible winners. We questioned each other, reacted, probed, enthused. By the end of the evening we had a shortlist of thirteen plays, this being exactly as many plays as there were people on the panel.

Our task now was to read the shortlist, so the agenda for the second meeting wrote itself: it was a simple matter of sharing our feelings about all thirteen plays, arguing in favor of those we loved and gently demurring over the plays that we felt more doubtful about. After a lot of debate, we had a decision.

It wasn't an easy one to make because, as we all agreed, we'd had an excellent year. Quite why it should be that some years produce more remarkable writing than others, I can't say: there seems to be no logic to it, yet it happens. As if to confirm our sunny opinion, all three of our chosen plays went on to be produced. One of the runners-up, Nina Segal's *In the Nighttime (Before the Sunrise)*, a delicately painful meditation on marriage and parenthood, appeared at the prestigious Gate Theatre in London, while the other runner-up, Sarah DeLappe's *The Wolves*, a dazzling portrait of a female teenage soccer team, was produced with vast success in New York, and, as I write, is about to be revived.

Utility, our winner, was also successfully produced in New York shortly after our judging debates, and I had the good luck to see a version of the same production, reconstituted by the original director with the original cast, when Emily Schwend was given her award at the Lincoln Center in November 2016. I had loved the play when I read it, but it was fascinating to see how much more it revealed in performance.

What had attracted me to the play when I first read it was its empathy with people surviving in a harshly capitalistic world: people who watch every cent, whose job security is pretty well nil, whose opinions (they feel) are mostly disregarded by their social superiors and whose lives are subject to decisions made not by them, but by their bosses and managers and by corporations. The constituency of Donald Trump, as many regard them now.

Their disempowerment runs all the way through the play. I won't easily forget the young woman, Amber, getting an explanation from the utility company that, while it makes a sort of sense, is pedantic and cold: it's the kind of managerial argot that keeps an unchallengeable distance between most people and the towers of privilege.

This accuracy about where people are positioned in their society in terms of power is essential to realistic drama: it's one of the things that distinguishes it from its feebler cousin, naturalism.

Another factor, and an essential one, is unflinching attention to the lives of women. Throughout its history, whenever drama has made a great move forward, it has done so by invoking greater realism. And whether this has been at the hand of Euripides, Shakespeare, or Ibsen, it has largely done so by putting women center-stage and endowing them with all the awakened consciousness that the playwright can summon up from the heart.

The character of Amber, the young woman and mother in *Utility*, is what struck me most freshly when I saw the play. The men in the play have charm, they do their best after a fashion, and one can imagine them being attractive, but it's clear that if Amber weren't holding the home and the family together, everything would collapse. What Schwend conveys so beautifully is that while Amber is put-upon, she isn't a victim; that while her goodwill is exploited, she isn't a mug; and that she has a sharp, clear vision of what is happening around her. If she keeps the home together, it isn't because she has to: it's because she knows that *somebody* has to and, like it or not, she has chosen to take it on.

It's a reliable sign of a good play that its theatrical effects, its "tools" if you like, are used in as many different ways as possible. A good example is when the electricity is cut off halfway through the play. The event has an obvious dramatic role. A party has been planned, the kids are looking forward to it: what will happen?

But there's a hint of metaphor to the darkness: once the power is cut off, disempowerment is suddenly very literal. And in a final twist, the lack of light releases the characters' emotions. As long as they see each other, they express their feelings in a guarded, conversational way. They may experience love, but they would run a mile from actually declaring it. But when the lights are out, things change: emotions are stripped naked, talk is franker. Hidden in darkness from his sister-in-law, the reticent, undemonstrative Jim expresses the love that, out of loyalty to his brother, he has suppressed ever since he met her. It's a rapt and exquisite moment and great theatre.

When our winner and runners-up were announced, there was some congratulatory comment in the New York press over the fact that all three were women: this followed a recent news story about the paucity of plays by women on Broadway. But as I've explained, the panel and I hadn't *known* they were written by women: we'd simply chosen what we thought were the best plays.

Here's one of them.

Nicholas Wright

Utility

Utility was first produced by The Amoralists at the Rattlestick Playwrights Theater in New York City on January 28, 2016. It was directed by Jay Stull and had a set by Kate Noll, lighting by Nicholas Houfek, sound by Jeanne Travis, costumes by Angela Harner, and props by Zach Serafin. The stage manager was Nikki Castle, and the production manager was Jeremy Pape. The cast was as follows:

AMBER   Vanessa Vache

CHRIS   James Kautz

JIM   Alex Grubbs

LAURA   Melissa Hurst

Characters
(2 Females, 2 Males)

AMBER   Only 31, but seems older. A not-so-secret smoker juggling two nearly full-time jobs and three kids, she is always exhausted and tapping into inner wells of strength to care for her family.

CHRIS   Amber's husband, 33. Charming as hell, eternally optimistic, and constantly in and out of work, but he means well.

JIM   Chris's brother, 36. A closed book, but a good one. Reliable and handy, but undateable, at least according to all of his ex-girlfriends.

LAURA   Amber's mother, 50. On the other side of world-weary, she's raised her kids and isn't looking to raise her grandchildren, but she's got some opinions anyway.

Time: Now

Place: The kitchen of a half-fixed-up house in East Texas
Briefly, the porch of Amber's mother's house down the block

Playwright's Note:
This play requires patience and time. The beats and silences in this script should be seen as a road map to both the pace of the play and the inner life of its characters, especially Amber. When a specific amount of time is noted in the script for a

particular moment, it is crucial to follow this instruction. Err on the side of more time rather than less, if there is ever a question. The success of the play depends on it.

There is no intermission.

Scene One

Evening.

AMBER *and* CHRIS *stand on the porch of* AMBER*'s mom's house.*

AMBER *is smoking a cigarette.*

CHRIS   Just seems like it makes more sense, that's all.

AMBER   Oh, that's all, huh?

CHRIS   No, I mean. Shit. This is coming out wrong.

AMBER   Yeah, all right, Chris. You still picking up the kids tomorrow morning?

CHRIS   Yeah, but don't change the subject. All right? Look. How many times we gonna go back and forth like this?

AMBER   Back and forth like what?

CHRIS   Like you want to get back together and I don't, and I want to get back together and you don't. And then, you know, in six months, I got someone else, and all of a sudden it's gonna be like, "Chris, we got the kids and I still love you and this and that."

AMBER   Oh, 'cause in six months, you gonna—you know what? You go ahead and find someone else wants to

handle all your shit. That is fine by me. 'Cause I am sick
and tired of it. And right now, you're feeling lonely and
you're broke, and you think this is gonna be the quick fix,
but it ain't the quick fix.

CHRIS   I don't think it's the quick fix.

AMBER   All right.

CHRIS   I don't. I really been thinking about it.

AMBER   All right.

CHRIS   Look. Just makes sense to me. That's all I'm
saying.

AMBER   Oh, that's all you're saying.

CHRIS   C'mon now. It'll be easier this way.

AMBER   Right. It'll be easier, 'til it ain't easier no more.

CHRIS   And also you still like me, even when you
pretend you hate me.

AMBER   'Cause I don't got the energy to hate you. I am
just done with the bullshit, okay? Every time, it's the same
thing.

CHRIS   Yeah, and every time, you say, "no no no," and
then three months later we're back together again or you
want to be back together again and I'm like "no way" and
so why don't we just cut the crap and do it right one time.

AMBER   What's that even mean, "do it right"? You
don't even know what that means.

CHRIS   I know what that means. And we can move back into the house.

AMBER   House still got all that water damage from the pipes. In the hallway and in the kitchen and in the kids' room, you forgetting that?

CHRIS   Well, what if I told you I'm fixing that up. For you.

AMBER   Since when can you fix a busted-up floor?

CHRIS   I can fix it.

AMBER   And mold in the walls.

CHRIS   And Jim's helping me, so.

AMBER   And it ain't even about the house, Chris. That ain't a reason to get back together with someone.

CHRIS   Well, it ain't the only reason.

AMBER   And there's a whole mess of reasons why we shouldn't get back together.

CHRIS   It'd be better for the kids. Don't gotta shuffle 'em around so much. I can pick 'em up. Drive 'em 'round for you. I can be home when you gotta go to the hospital late.

AMBER   You got a car I don't know about?

CHRIS   I could wait with Janie at the bus stop so you don't gotta drop her off early no more. Or I could bring Max and Sammy to that day care you send 'em to. Or whatever else you need. Run errands. Help out. Plus, I'm picking up shifts at JJ's now, so that's a help. A few times a week.

AMBER   Oh, yeah?

CHRIS   A couple times a week.

AMBER   I hate that place.

CHRIS   Well.

A beat.

AMBER *is considering it.*

AMBER   What about Dakota?

CHRIS   She lives with her mom now in Oklahoma, so. And she's fourteen. And it ain't like I can afford child support, so.

AMBER   If you could afford child support, I better be seeing all of that. Day care just went up to thirty dollars a week for the two of them. Each.

CHRIS   Well, if I can stay home with 'em, you won't need to send 'em to day care so much.

AMBER   That's a big if.

CHRIS   It ain't a big if.

AMBER   You could stay with 'em now, if you like. Don't got nothing to do about us getting back together.

CHRIS   Sure it does.

AMBER   Not really. You want to see the kids more, you go right ahead. You got keys to my mom's, right? You stop by you want. And you know what else? I dunno why you're talking all about JJ's like that's gonna be some kinda thing gonna convince me.

CHRIS   She ain't even working there no more.

AMBER   Tsst.

CHRIS   And it wouldn't be a problem if she was, so.

A beat.

AMBER   It's late, Chris.

CHRIS   I know.

AMBER   I gotta go to work in like. Five minutes ago.

CHRIS   I know, just. Listen to me.

AMBER   What.

CHRIS   I'm a different person now. Hey, look at me. I'm a different person. I kicked the pills. For real this time. Last Christmas. Ain't had a single slip-up.

AMBER   Not yet.

CHRIS   And I ain't gonna.

AMBER   I don't know, Chris. I don't want to get the kids' hopes up just to get disappointed again.

CHRIS   Listen.

(beat)
When I was walking home tonight after I dropped the
kids off, my mind was all. I dunno. My mind was racing
like a mile a minute, and I just felt like. I don't know. Like
it wasn't right. Seeing 'em a little bit here, a little bit there.
Seeing you for five seconds when you get home. Talking
to your ma like there ain't nothing wrong with it all and
then walking to my brother's house and sleeping on his
couch. While our house is empty and flooded out and
falling apart. We should fix it. We should move back in.
You and me and the kids.

AMBER   Even if the house was fixed up—

CHRIS   It's gonna be. I'm telling you. We're almost
done with the kitchen now, and when that's done we can
move back in, so. Kids can sleep in the living room for a
bit. And I know that ain't perfect, but it's gotta be better
than your ma's living room. All of you in one room, that
any better?

AMBER   Least we know what we're coming home to
every day.

CHRIS   And I miss you. All of you.
   (beat)
   Hey.

AMBER   What.

CHRIS   Hey, c'mere.

AMBER *doesn't.*

CHRIS (cont'd)   Come over here.

She still doesn't, so he goes over to her.

CHRIS (cont'd)   It's gonna be good this time.

AMBER   You don't know that.

CHRIS   I do know that. I'm telling you that 'cause I
know that to be a fact.

AMBER   You don't know that, Chris.

He wraps his arms around her, and she lets him.

CHRIS   I do know that. I know it. I swear.

Scene Two

Three months later.

The kitchen of CHRIS *and* AMBER*'s mostly fixed-up house.*

It's so early it barely seems like morning yet.

AMBER *is making lunches for her kids. She's wearing scrubs and is fresh off a night shift. Exhausted.*

Suddenly, loud thumps against the back door make her jump.

AMBER   Jesus Christ.

A beat.

Then JIM, CHRIS*'s older brother, enters. He sets a toolbox on the floor next to him.*

AMBER (cont'd)   You gotta thump your boots on the door like that? The kids are still sleeping.

JIM   You said you don't like it I track mud in the house.

AMBER   You never heard of a doormat? Wipe your feet on it? Gotta bang on the back door at five o'clock in the morning, wake up the whole neighborhood?

JIM   You want to fix me one of those?

AMBER   These are for the kids. You want something to eat, there's leftover wings in the fridge.

JIM   Hot wings at five in the morning, shit.

AMBER   I seen you do worse.

JIM   Chris up yet?

AMBER   No. You want coffee or something?

JIM   If you're offering.

AMBER   I just offered. That is what I just did.

JIM   Then all right.

She fills a mug with water, puts it in the microwave.

AMBER   You coming for Janie's birthday party tomorrow?

JIM   I dunno. Maybe.

AMBER   She'd like that.

JIM   I mean. I don't think she'd really care. I didn't go to her party last year.

AMBER   'Cause she didn't have a party last year.

JIM   Well.

AMBER   And Janie likes you. She still talks about that time you brought her and Maxie that helicopter toy. The one got stuck on the roof, but.

JIM   Well. What kinda party is it gonna be?

AMBER   A children's party, Jim.

JIM   Yeah, I dunno.

AMBER   You know what? Fine. Don't come.

JIM   Her dad gonna be there?

AMBER   I invited him, but I ain't heard back.

JIM   Oh.

AMBER   And Chris don't like him, so it's probably better he ain't coming anyway.

JIM   I guess so.

AMBER   It ain't just gonna be kids. Neighbors coming, too. Some of the parents of the other kids.

JIM   I'll think about it.

AMBER   Whatever, Jim.

A beat.

AMBER *goes back to fixing lunches.*

JIM   Your mom gonna be there?

AMBER   Yeah, she's gonna be there.

JIM   Your mom don't like me.

AMBER   Well, that ain't true.

JIM   Well, that is true, but.

AMBER   And how much time you ever spent with my mom anyway?

JIM   Here and there.

AMBER   Name one time that ain't just.

JIM   I dunno.

AMBER   Running into her at the house, or.

JIM   At your wedding.

AMBER   That was six years ago.

JIM   And here and there.

AMBER   Jim, I don't know what you're talking about.

JIM   Talking about she don't like me.

The microwave beeps.

AMBER *takes out the mug of water and stirs in instant coffee. Hands it to* JIM.

AMBER   So you got a problem with my mom now?

JIM   Nah. Just sayin'.

AMBER   Just sayin'.

JIM   Forget it. I'll make an appearance.

AMBER   Oh, great. That is just so kind of you, Jim, I swear to Christ. You want milk, it's in the fridge.

JIM *drinks the coffee black.*

JIM   How old's she gonna be?

AMBER   Eight.

JIM   What kinda present you get for an eight-year-old girl?

AMBER   You could get her a book or a game or—why don't I get something for her and you pay me back and then that's what you give her?

JIM   All right.

AMBER   I want it to be nice for her. I'm getting one of those huge sheet cakes from Walmart and there's gonna be a piñata full of candy. And I hired a clown to make balloon animals for all the kids.

JIM   Clowns give me the creeps.

AMBER   That's what everyone says.

JIM   Can't be what everyone says. That's the case, there wouldn't be no clowns.

CHRIS *enters in a t-shirt and gym shorts, yawning.*

CHRIS   Holy shit. You ain't kidding you said you'd get here early.

JIM   Gotta be in Tyler at eleven, so.

CHRIS *takes half a sandwich from the pile on the counter.*

AMBER   Those are for the kids!

CHRIS   Janie don't like turkey, so.

AMBER   Well, I don't care if she don't like it, 'cause that's what she's getting today. It's good for her. It's healthy.

JIM   Don't they give 'em lunch at school?

AMBER   Not for free. And it's all french fries and that sorta thing.

JIM   Lunch ain't free for kids no more?

AMBER   You can send in a form to get like a voucher, but we missed the cutoff so now we gotta wait 'til next year. And those women work in the cafeteria are just miserable pieces of shit. Tell those kids don't got it paid for they can't have lunch—right in front of everyone— 'cause they don't got the balance on their account. Take the trays right outta their hands.

JIM   I dated a woman worked in a school cafeteria once.

AMBER   Oh yeah?

JIM   She just cooked in the back, though. I dunno if she was turning no kids away from the lunch line.

CHRIS   We got juice in the fridge?

AMBER   Just juice boxes for the kids and don't you dare drink none of 'em.

CHRIS *goes to* AMBER, *teasing.*

CHRIS   You came home cranky today!

AMBER   Cut it out, Chris, I ain't in no mood.

CHRIS   Why don't you go on to bed then? You got a few hours.

AMBER   'Cause I got shit to do today, and if I go to sleep now I might just never wake up again.

CHRIS   And then where would I be?

AMBER   Nowhere good.

CHRIS   There's coffee?

AMBER   Yeah, but there ain't creamer. We ran out yesterday.

CHRIS   Well, shoot.

AMBER   Yep.

CHRIS *fixes himself a cup of coffee.*

CHRIS   Christ, it's early. Sun ain't even up yet.

JIM   Starting to be.

CHRIS   I remember when we used to stay up 'til sunrise and then we'd drive through McDonald's for the breakfast menu and sneak past Ma before she left for work in the morning. Sleep for the next six hours. Sleep through my first couple classes.

JIM   Probably wasn't the best idea.

CHRIS   Ma never found out, though.

JIM   Well. She did, but.

AMBER   Chris, will you wake Max up? He needs a five-minute warning these days, or everyone's running fifteen minutes late.

CHRIS   All right.
   (toward the living room)
   MAX, WAKE YOUR ASS UP!

AMBER   Goddammit, Chris.

She shoves the sandwiches in brown paper bags and goes to wake the kids properly.

CHRIS   What'd you say to her?

JIM   Nothing.

CHRIS   She's in a mood.

JIM   Well.

CHRIS   Hey, you still seeing that girl works at that ice cream place?

JIM   Nope.

CHRIS   Ah, shoot.

JIM   Saw her with some twenty-something someone or other at the 7-Eleven.

CHRIS   Fucking twenty-something someones.

JIM   Well she's a twenty-something someone, so.

CHRIS   Well, sorry, man.

JIM   I think I forgot to text her anyway, so.

CHRIS   Eh, she ain't worth the trouble.

JIM   Why you asking?

CHRIS   I was gonna see if you could get some ice cream for the party tomorrow. Amber tell you about it?

JIM   Yeah, I said I'd go.

CHRIS   Hey, you know, one of Janie's friends got a single mom kinda situation. She's all right.

JIM   Nah.

CHRIS   Just sayin'.

JIM   You want, I could pick up some ice cream for you anyway. Make it a birthday present.

CHRIS   Yeah? 'Cause I told Amber I'd get decorations and paper plates and all that, too. And I been a bit light these days.

JIM   You ask 'em to give you Saturday nights at JJ's?

CHRIS   Yeah, but. Everyone wants Saturday night. Only way to make a living there.

JIM   You ain't gonna make a living there.

CHRIS   Well.

AMBER *returns with a tiny child's backpack. She stuffs a lunch inside, zips it up.*

AMBER   Don't forget—you gotta pick up Janie today 'cause I gotta be at Wingstop at 10:30.

CHRIS   She told me she wants to take the bus home.

AMBER   Well, she can't take the bus home 'cause Max got a doctor's appointment at 3:45 and you ain't gonna be here to let her in the house.

CHRIS   I hate going to the doctor.

AMBER   Well, it ain't for you. They said he don't get his booster shots this week he can't go to day care.

CHRIS   There's gas in the tank?

AMBER   Yeah, 'cause I put ten dollars into it. You left it running on empty last night, I don't even know how long. I had to pull into an Exxon station three exits early and I was late to work.

CHRIS   There's the gas station right here on the corner, you coulda just stopped there. Wouldn't take you more than a second.

AMBER Well, I didn't notice it 'til I was already on I-20, so I couldn't just stop there.

CHRIS Also that car can run on empty for a while. You coulda got there no problem.

AMBER Yeah, so it might stall out on the highway? Anyway. You gotta get both the boys at three at day care and then Janie at 3:20 when she's out of class.

CHRIS All right. You want me to drop you off at work first?

AMBER Ain't worth it.

CHRIS Suit yourself.

JIM You want, I can give you a ride on my way to Tyler.

AMBER Yeah?

JIM On my way. No skin off my back.

AMBER Well, maybe I'll take you up on that. And Chris, make sure the kids got their seatbelts on, 'cause that car been acting funny lately.

CHRIS 'Course I make sure they wear their seatbelts, I mean, shit.

AMBER *heads out of the kitchen.*

AMBER *(to the kids)* Y'all better be out of those beds now!

She disappears into the living room.

CHRIS   Goddamn, she is in a mood today.

JIM   Well.
   (beat)
   Ran into Michelle last night.

CHRIS *glances toward the living room.*

CHRIS   Oh yeah?

JIM   Asked about you.

CHRIS   What'd you say?

JIM *shrugs.*

CHRIS (cont'd)   Tsst.

JIM   Seems like she didn't know you was back with
Amber there.

CHRIS   Well, I ain't seen Michelle in a while.

JIM   All right.

CHRIS   I mean. She sends me texts from time to time.

JIM   You send her texts back?

CHRIS   Not really.

JIM   All right.

CHRIS   Not in any real kinda way.

JIM   All right, you gotta be careful about that.

CHRIS   Ain't nothing there to be careful about.

JIM   If you say so.

CHRIS   I mean. She's trouble.

JIM   Yep.
(beat)
Yep. You know, she said she's gonna start at JJ's again.

CHRIS   Oh yeah?

JIM   Yeah.

CHRIS   Well, shit.

JIM   Thought you mighta heard.

CHRIS   Nah, they don't tell me nothin'.

JIM   Anyway, that's what she said. They kept cutting her hours at the Arby's and then calling her in last minute. Said she'd rather work less hours and know when they are than keep the whole day free just in case.

CHRIS   Well. I guess that makes sense.

JIM   Yup.

CHRIS   Don't tell that to Amber, all right?

JIM   Yeah, whatever, man.

CHRIS   Trouble with a capital T, I tell you what.

JIM   Time is it?

CHRIS   Hell if I know. Too early.

JIM   Drink up, we got drywall to hang.

CHRIS   Can't rush a man in the morning.

JIM   I told you I gotta be in Tyler at eleven, and that ain't gonna change we're halfway done the wall and you're asking me, you know. Stay a few minutes 'til the job's done.

CHRIS   Jesus Christ, all right.

JIM   No skin off my back you got a house full of mold.

CHRIS   I thought we already got most of the mold.

JIM   I ain't staying late is all I'm sayin'.

CHRIS   All right, all right. Let me throw on a pair of jeans and my boots.

And CHRIS *dumps his cup of coffee in the sink and goes into the living room.*

JIM *finishes his coffee and puts the mug in the sink. He goes to the backpacks on the counter, zips them up. Then he grabs his toolbox and exits.*

Scene Three

Later that morning.

Noise from another room as CHRIS *and* JIM *fix the bedroom.*

Keys in the door. AMBER *comes into the kitchen, carrying shopping bags from Walmart and balancing a large white cake box in one hand.*

She is on her cell phone, which is balanced against her ear.

AMBER   No, 'cause if you come by later, she might be here and I don't want her seeing everything. . . . No, 'cause I hid it all and I don't want her to . . . Mom. Mom, I only got like twenty minutes before I gotta go to— . . . yeah, exactly, so can you please come over while she ain't here? It'll take you less than two minutes to drive down the block. Please . . . Okay . . . Yeah, I'll be here.

She hangs up the phone.

As she goes to set down the Walmart bags, the cake box slides out of her hand and crashes to the floor.

AMBER (cont'd)   Shit!

She stares at the cake box.

AMBER (cont'd)   Shit. Shit. Shit.

She nervously opens the lid of the box.

The cake is all smashed up.

AMBER (cont'd)   Oh, God fucking dammit.

She picks the box up and puts it on the counter.

She looks at the ruined cake for a moment.

She gets a knife out of a drawer and tries to fix the cake.

It doesn't work.

AMBER (cont'd)   Oh, Christ. Great. That's great.

She folds the lid back over the box and puts the whole thing in the refrigerator.

A beat.

AMBER *lights up a cigarette. She smokes.*

She goes into the living room, returns with a tube of wrapping paper.

She searches in a junk drawer for scissors, tape.

She takes a small toy out of the Walmart bag and starts wrapping it.

She hears a car pull into the drive.

Moments later, LAURA, AMBER*'s mother, appears at the back door and lets herself in the kitchen.*

LAURA   You got tea in the fridge?

AMBER   Yeah, we got tea. Where's the bicycle?

LAURA   It's in the backseat of my car, where you think it is?

AMBER *goes out to* LAURA*'s car.*

LAURA *fixes herself a glass of iced tea, sits down at the table.*

AMBER (off)   How did you get this in here?

LAURA   I don't know, Amber, I just did.

A beat.

LAURA *drinks tea.*

Another beat.

LAURA (cont'd)   You get it out of there?
        (*beat*)
I don't want to drive around with a bicycle in the backseat of my car all day.

AMBER (off)   Yeah, I got it!

AMBER *returns to the kitchen, pushing a white and pink bicycle.*

A loud noise from the kids' room.

LAURA   What in the lord's name is that sound?

AMBER   They're fixing up the kids' room. All of 'em still sleeping in the living room.

LAURA   When you were Janie's age, you slept in my room with me, you remember that?

AMBER   I remember, Mom.
    (beat)
    They like spending the night on your fold-out couch. Janie says it's like a slumber party.

LAURA   Is that what she says?

AMBER *(re: the bicycle)*   Wish I had one of them giant bows to put on it. Well.

AMBER *sets the bicycle next to the door.*

LAURA *sips the tea.*

LAURA   This unsweetened tea?

AMBER   No, it's got sugar.

LAURA   It ain't sweetened like how I like it sweetened.

AMBER   Well, I dunno how you like it sweetened, Mom.

LAURA   It's sweetened like how you like it sweetened, I guess.

AMBER   You can add more sugar if you want to.

LAURA   It's like chewing on a tea leaf.

AMBER   Or there's Sweet'N Low in the cabinet.

AMBER *starts wrapping presents at the table again.*

LAURA   When the kids get home, then?

AMBER   Not for a while.

LAURA   'Cause you gotta make sure she don't see none of this.

AMBER   I know, Mom, that's why I'm wrapping 'em now.

LAURA   You don't want 'em coming home in the middle of—

AMBER   They're at school, Mom. And day care. And they gotta go to the doctor after school, anyway, so they ain't gonna be home 'til—

LAURA   What're they going to the doctor for?

AMBER   It's just for Max.

LAURA   What's wrong with Max?

AMBER   Nothing. Just booster shots.

LAURA   You hear that thing about vaccinations on the radio the other day?

AMBER   I don't listen to the radio, Mom.

LAURA   They were saying kids getting sick from all these shots we're giving 'em.

AMBER   Well, if they don't get their shots, they can get hepatitis, so.

LAURA   I dunno, Amber. I just know I don't like them telling me what to do with our kids.

AMBER   Who's them, Mom?

LAURA *(darkly)*   You know.

AMBER   Well, they ain't your kids, Mom. They're my kids. And all of 'em gotten all their shots and none of 'em ever got sick from none of 'em.

LAURA   I'm just sayin'. Don't seem right to me. You know there was a doctor talking about it, and he was saying that medicine is all a big crapshoot. And they don't really know what's gonna work and why and what ain't gonna work and why not.

AMBER   Well, they know vaccinations work 'cause all of a sudden we don't got polio no more, so.

LAURA   And we ain't had none of these new vaccinations around long enough to see what the, ah. Long-term effects gonna be.

AMBER   Well, we know what the long-term effects of hepatitis are, Mom, so. So I guess I'll take my chances with a vaccination.

LAURA   They even got a vaccination for chicken pox now.

AMBER   I know, Mom. I got it for the kids.

A beat.

LAURA   When you were a little girl, there was a boy down the block who had chicken pox and I just sent you over there so you would catch it from him.

AMBER   That's terrible.

LAURA   No, it is not, Amber. That is what they told us to do. 'Cause if you catch chicken pox when you're young, it ain't a big deal. Chicken pox is just some itchy spots and a fever. But if you don't get it when you're young, you can have a whole world of trouble you catch that as an adult, and that is the truth.

AMBER   All right, Mom.

LAURA   And you were gonna be home anyway because it was summer vacation, so you didn't even miss a day of school.

AMBER   Well. Fantastic. That is great planning.

They wrap presents for a moment.

LAURA   You're giving that girl a pack of chewing gum for her birthday?

AMBER   She likes chewing gum.

LAURA   When you were a little girl, I didn't let none of that stuff in the house.

AMBER   I know, Mom.

LAURA   You try getting gum out of the carpet.

AMBER   She ain't gonna get it in the carpet.

LAURA   And if she gives a piece to the boys, you'll have
real trouble.

AMBER   She ain't gonna give it to the boys.

LAURA   Chewing gum in their hair. You just try getting
that out. You remember when Jason got chewing gum in
his hair?

AMBER   No, 'cause I wasn't born yet.

LAURA   Well, I told you about it.

AMBER   Yeah, you told me about it.

LAURA   A real mess.

AMBER   I bet.

A beat.

LAURA   You hear from him lately?

AMBER   Not lately.

LAURA   He left me a message on my cell phone
yesterday.

AMBER   Why didn't you answer?

LAURA   Two days ago. It didn't ring.

AMBER   It didn't ring?

LAURA   Just went straight to the voice mail. I saw it
blinking.

AMBER   What did he say?

LAURA   Is there some way you can leave a message on someone's phone without letting the phone ring?

AMBER   I don't think so.

LAURA   I know I had it switched on but I dunno how all that works.

AMBER   What did he say?

LAURA   Oh, you know.
(beat)
I liked things before there was cell phones.

AMBER   Well, no one's making you have one.

LAURA *(re: the presents)*   You're making a mess of that. Give it here.

She takes the wrapping paper from AMBER, *who lets her.*

AMBER   I ain't seen him since the Fourth of July when he brought those fireworks and almost blew his thumb off.

LAURA   He came around in August, but he was just picking up that old dining room table.

AMBER   He ask you for grandma's ring yet?

LAURA   No, and I ain't gonna give it to him if he does ask for it.

AMBER   Really?

LAURA   I don't want that ring going out of the family. I'll give it to Janie when she's old enough to have it.

AMBER   Jason ain't gonna like that.

LAURA   Well, my mother wouldn't like it, that woman walking around with that ring on her finger.

AMBER   She's not so bad.

LAURA   Well.

AMBER   And I dunno he can do much better.

LAURA   Oh, he can do a lot better. That woman?

AMBER   Remember what's-her-face from high school? That girl he took to homecoming?

LAURA   Well, we knew he wasn't gonna end up with her!

AMBER   Still. He's done worse, is my point.

LAURA   Well, her family's got money. She don't need my mama's ring.

AMBER   So don't give it to him, Mom. I dunno.

LAURA   What is this?

She holds up a toy.

AMBER   It's a plastic hamburger.

LAURA   What is she gonna do with a plastic hamburger?

AMBER   It's got a sucker thing on it. You can stick it on like. The fridge or whatever. The bathtub.

LAURA   Well, what's she gonna do with a hamburger sucker?

AMBER   I don't know, Mom. She's gonna stick it on things. I wanted to have some stuff for her to open up.

LAURA   Last weekend, there was a yard sale at that house on, ah. Where was it?

AMBER   I had the kids all weekend.

LAURA   On North Street and something.

AMBER   Chris was helping his dad move out of his apartment.

LAURA   By the post office.

AMBER   Yeah, well, I had the kids all weekend.

LAURA   Why was his dad moving out of his apartment?

AMBER   He just couldn't stay there no more. I dunno.

JIM *enters. He's covered in dust and dirt.*

JIM   Oh, hey Mrs. Larson, I didn't know you were here.

AMBER   Mom brought over the bicycle.

JIM   Yeah, okay.

AMBER   You still going to Tyler in a bit?

JIM   I was fixing on it. Gotta stop at the house first.

AMBER   Okay.

JIM   Pick up some tools I left there.

LAURA   Y'all going somewhere?

AMBER   Jim's giving me a ride to Wingstop.

JIM   It's on my way.

LAURA   On your way to where?

JIM   On my way to Tyler.

LAURA   Didn't you say you gotta stop at your house first?

JIM   Yeah.

LAURA   Don't seem like it's on your way.

JIM   Well.

AMBER   Mom, what are you going on about it for?

LAURA   Don't make sense this boy driving all around town to here and there.

AMBER   Well, what do you care about it?

LAURA   I can give you a ride if you need a ride.

AMBER   You hate driving. I had to beg you to drive down the block just now.

LAURA   You did not.

AMBER   Okay. Whatever.

LAURA   And I gotta go to the Food Lion in any case, so. So it actually is on my way.

AMBER   Well. I guess it ain't like I'm gonna complain about two people wanting to give me a ride.
  (to JIM*)*
  Thanks anyway.

JIM   Doesn't matter to me.

He goes.

A beat.

LAURA   What time you gotta be there?

AMBER   Ten thirty.

LAURA   Who wants hot wings at 10:30 in the morning?

AMBER   It's open at eleven. I just gotta be there at ten thirty.

LAURA   I guess that's a little better.

A beat.

They continue wrapping the presents.

LAURA (cont'd)   You know. It's a good thing, Chris back living with y'all in this house.

AMBER   You think so?

LAURA   And good for the kids.

AMBER   Yeah, I guess.

LAURA   I know he ain't perfect, but.

AMBER   That's a real interesting way to put it.

LAURA   Well, you just try and raise up those three kids by yourself.

AMBER   Mom, who do you think pays most of the bills around here? Gets those kids dressed and fed almost every day? Ain't Chris.

LAURA   He does a lot around here.

AMBER   If you say so.

LAURA   He does a lot around here, Amber, I seen it with my own eyes. Running errands for 'em, fixing up their room for 'em, picking 'em up after school.

AMBER   Okay, Mom.

LAURA *finishes up the last present.*

LAURA   Well, that's the last of it. It's still only a deck of playing cards in there, but at least it looks all right.

AMBER   She likes playing cards.

LAURA   Well.

A beat.

AMBER   Mom?

LAURA   What?

A beat.

AMBER *changes her mind.*

AMBER   Can you come by early tomorrow? In case I
need help setting up?

LAURA   What time?

AMBER   I dunno. Sometime in the morning. Whenever
you can.

LAURA   I guess I don't got anything I gotta do tomorrow morning.

AMBER   Great, so.

LAURA   What do you got for decorating?

AMBER   I dunno. I think we got some balloons or
whatever.

LAURA   I got those Christmas tree lights up in the attic.

AMBER   Christmas tree lights?

LAURA   You can string 'em up around the house.
Around the backyard.

AMBER   You don't think it'll look too much like Christmas?

LAURA   Kids like Christmas.

AMBER   I guess so.
   (beat)
   I just want it to be special. Feels like it should be a special thing. Eight years old. I dunno.

LAURA   Kids don't know the difference. Long as there's cake and toys and presents.

AMBER   I know the difference.

LAURA   Well. Ain't a party for you.

AMBER   I know, just. Forget it.

LAURA   Well.

AMBER   Where am I gonna hide that bike?

LAURA   Put it in the kids' room. They ain't allowed in there while it's getting fixed up, right?

AMBER   Ha. I guess that's right.

AMBER *puts her glass in the sink.*

A beat.

Then she goes over to the bike and starts to wheel it out to the kids' room.

AMBER (cont'd)   You about ready to go?

LAURA   What else I gotta do here?

AMBER   Okay.

AMBER *exits with the bike.*

LAURA *sits at the table for another moment, alone.*

Scene Four

Evening.

The bicycle is gone, hidden from Janie. The kitchen floor is covered with balloons.

CHRIS *is blowing up a balloon. He goes to tie it off, but the balloon escapes and flies out of his hand.*

CHRIS   Goddamned fucking balloon.

He takes another balloon, blows it up.

AMBER *enters with some grocery bags. She's wearing her Wingstop uniform, and she's finishing the last of a cigarette.*

AMBER   Give me a hand, Chris?

CHRIS   Just a second.

AMBER   Marnie is outside in the drive waiting on me to get these groceries outta her car.

CHRIS   Hang on, I almost got it.

He struggles to tie off the balloon.

AMBER   Never goddamned mind.

She drops the bags on the table, goes back to the car.

CHRIS *continues to struggle to tie the balloon.*

CHRIS   What is wrong with these balloons?

AMBER *returns with another armful of groceries.*

CHRIS *finally ties the balloon.*

AMBER   Christ, I am too tired to think. Kids asleep?

CHRIS   Boys are. I dunno about Janie. I let her sleep in our room. She wanted to stay up and read some of that book your mom gave her.

AMBER   All right. Anything left from dinner?

CHRIS   Eh, I got 'em Whataburger.

AMBER   We already got hamburger thawed in the fridge!

CHRIS   I know, but. I thought a treat after the doctor and all.

AMBER   They're gonna have a million treats tomorrow.

CHRIS   Well, now they got one more. They don't get a lot of treats, anyhow.

AMBER   You see the cake?

CHRIS   Yeah, looks great.

AMBER   Well, then you didn't see it. All smashed up.

CHRIS   How's that now?

AMBER   I dropped it.

CHRIS   Well. Kids ain't gonna care what it looks like, they'll be so hopped up on sugar.

AMBER *throws a load of laundry into the washer.*

AMBER   Well, I care what it looks like. Looks like I dug it out of the dumpster in the back of the Walmart.

CHRIS   It don't look like that.

AMBER   You don't know what it looks like, you ain't seen it. You said it looks great two seconds ago.

CHRIS   All right, I am over these balloons, man. You want to blow up some balloons, you be my guest, 'cause I am done.

AMBER   You get plastic plates and forks and all that?

CHRIS   Yes, ma'am.

AMBER   Napkins?

CHRIS   Yes, ma'am.

AMBER   Candles for the cake?

CHRIS   They're on the table there.

AMBER   Okay. Then I guess you got everything.

CHRIS   Do you think I should—

AMBER   Cups for the kids?

CHRIS   What?

AMBER   You get cups for the kids to drink out of?

CHRIS   Don't we got cups?

AMBER   How're we gonna give kids Kool-Aid without giving 'em cups to drink it out of?

CHRIS   They wasn't on the list!

AMBER   I know I put cups on the list.

CHRIS   I'll go get 'em in the morning.

AMBER   Nah, I'll just run out now.

CHRIS   Nuh uh. You're spinning. You sit there at the table.

AMBER   Chris, it'll take me twenty minutes.

CHRIS   All right, then it'll take me twenty minutes tomorrow morning. Sit down.

AMBER   And I gotta put up the groceries.

CHRIS   I'll do it. Go on, I ain't telling you twice.

AMBER *sits at the table.*

CHRIS *starts to put up the groceries.*

CHRIS (cont'd)   Want me to heat up this leftover macaroni we got in here?

AMBER   Okay.

CHRIS   And there's some of that broccoli with the cheese sauce, you want that.

AMBER   Okay.

CHRIS   Okay.

CHRIS *puts the macaroni and broccoli in the microwave, and goes back to the groceries.*

AMBER   You think these balloons gonna look stupid?

CHRIS   Hey, I worked hard on those balloons!

AMBER   Balloons are supposed to float in the air not just. Sit on the floor in a heap.

CHRIS   They'll look fine. Kids can, you know. Kick 'em around.

AMBER   They had balloons for sale at the Walmart. Like balloons that can actually float in the air like balloons are supposed to do. I shoulda bought a couple. Just for outside. Tie 'em on the mailbox or something.

CHRIS   I think these look real good. Like a ball pit. But with balloons.

AMBER   I dunno.

CHRIS   Balloon pit. Maybe the clown can do something with 'em.

AMBER   There ain't gonna be a clown.

CHRIS   Why not?

AMBER   'Cause he was gonna charge us three hours and gas money even though it says on his website it's just twenty dollars an hour and it doesn't say nothing about a three-hour minimum or gas money. So.

CHRIS   Well, you know what? Good. Clowns creep me out.

AMBER   Ha.

CHRIS   What?

AMBER   Jim said the same thing this morning.

CHRIS   Well. Ain't that what everyone says about clowns?

AMBER   That's what I said.

CHRIS   Dunno why there's even still clowns.

AMBER   Well. Everyone can't think that, I guess. Otherwise there wouldn't be no clowns.

CHRIS   Guess not.

AMBER   Kids woulda liked it.

CHRIS   Bet he was a piece of shit clown in any case. Better off.

AMBER   Jim was giving me shit this morning.

CHRIS   Kids don't even like clowns.

AMBER   You hear me?

CHRIS   What're you talking about Jim?

He takes her dinner out of the microwave.

CHRIS (cont'd)   It's hot, so be careful.

AMBER   Just. He always gotta be a big pill.

CHRIS   Nah.

AMBER   Yeah.

CHRIS   That's just Jim.

AMBER   Whatever.

CHRIS   That's just how he is.

AMBER   That's just how he is to me. I know he didn't want you moving back here with me.

CHRIS   No way. He was ready for me to get off his couch, that is the truth.

AMBER   That ain't the same thing as wanting you back here with me and the kids.

CHRIS   I don't think he thinks all that hard about it.

AMBER   Got an attitude on him when he walks through the door. And I can't say nothing 'cause he's doing us a favor.

CHRIS   Nah.

AMBER   Yeah.

A beat.

CHRIS   I think you're reading into shit the way you like to read into shit sometimes, so.

AMBER   Oh, that's what you think?

CHRIS   That's what I think. And he's coming over tomorrow morning to finish up the kids' room, and would he do that if he had some sorta problem with you? With us?

AMBER   Probably. He's your brother, so what's he gonna do, say no?

CHRIS   He could. But he doesn't have a problem, so.

CHRIS *gets a text message, and he toys with his phone for a moment, then leaves it on the counter.*

AMBER *clocks all of this.*

AMBER   Where'd you put the records from the doctor?

CHRIS   They said they'd fax 'em over to the day care.

AMBER   They always say that and then they never do it and that's why you gotta get copies. 'Cause what're we gonna do on Monday morning when the day care says they ain't got 'em and Max can't stay there? You gonna wake up early and watch him all day? Tell 'em you can't pick up a shift if they call you in for the afternoon?

CHRIS   I'll go over to the doctor's office tomorrow and pick 'em up.

AMBER   They ain't open on the weekend.

CHRIS   Then I'll go on Monday morning if they ain't faxed 'em. But she promised they would, so.

AMBER   They always say that, and then they don't.

CHRIS   Well. Then I'll watch Max on Monday and pick up the records myself, there ain't nothing to worry about.

AMBER *picks at the macaroni.*

AMBER   You working tomorrow night?

CHRIS   Nah, they ain't giving me Saturdays.

AMBER   'Cause the party's gonna wind down before dinner.

CHRIS   Well, I don't got work tomorrow, so.

AMBER   Sherry says they need a bartender at the Chili's in Lindale.

CHRIS   Who's Sherry?

AMBER   From work. Her husband is a waiter there.

CHRIS   Long drive.

AMBER   Better money.

CHRIS   Yeah, maybe.

AMBER   Can't hurt. See if he'll put in a good word for you.

CHRIS   He doesn't know me.

AMBER   I'll ask Sherry.

CHRIS   Sherry doesn't know me.

AMBER   Then, all right, you keep working like two hours a week at JJ's. We sure got money to burn around here.

CHRIS   I'll apply. I'm just saying. It's far away so I'll always need the car. And they don't hire people like me.

AMBER   Well, I don't know what that's supposed to mean.

CHRIS   And I kinda like working at JJ's.

AMBER   You barely work there.

CHRIS   Well.

AMBER   And I hate it. I hate that you work there.

CHRIS   Well.

A beat.

CHRIS *watches* AMBER *picking at the macaroni.*

CHRIS (cont'd)   Eat that. Now it's gonna get cold.

AMBER *takes a bite.*

CHRIS (cont'd)   You want me to put all these balloons in the yard tomorrow morning?

AMBER   That's gonna look stupid.

CHRIS   Nah, it ain't gonna look stupid. Hey, you know what I can do? I can tape them up on the cabinets and like. All around the house.

AMBER   That will definitely look stupid.

CHRIS   Nah, it'll look fine. And I can scatter some of them around the porch or something.

He opens a cabinet under the sink.

AMBER   They're gonna get balloon pieces all over.

CHRIS   Well, that ain't the worst thing. We out of trash bags?

AMBER   No, they're in the back there.

CHRIS *roots around, finds the trash bags.*

CHRIS *takes out a trash bag, then looks around at all the balloons.*

CHRIS   We got bigger trash bags?

AMBER   No, that's what we got, why?

CHRIS   'Cause I was gonna stuff all these balloons in a trash bag so they ain't in the way all day tomorrow, but. I dunno, how many balloons you think I can fit in here?

AMBER   I dunno, Chris.

CHRIS   Maybe it's a stupid idea.

AMBER   Well, those balloons gonna look stupid no matter what.

CHRIS   They ain't gonna look—

Suddenly, the lights go out.

AMBER   Well, goddammit.

CHRIS   What in the hell?

AMBER   Goddammit, Chris.

CHRIS   What, I didn't do it!

AMBER   Are the other houses on the block out too?

CHRIS *stumbles to the kitchen window.*

CHRIS   Doesn't look like it.

AMBER *rummages through a drawer and gets a flashlight.*

AMBER   Goddammit. We got til the end of the month to pay the bill.

CHRIS   I dunno.

AMBER   We got til the end of the month, that's what they always say.

CHRIS   Yeah, I dunno.

AMBER   I mean. You paid the minimum last week, right?

CHRIS   What's that?

AMBER   It's like twenty-five bucks. You paid that, right?
I told you to send them a check.

CHRIS   Oh, shit.

AMBER   Oh shit what.

CHRIS   I guess I spent that on Janie's sleeping bag.

AMBER   I told you she didn't need that!

CHRIS   She just had that old blanket. Sheets from her
bed. The boys have sleeping bags.

AMBER   Well, now she needs there to be lights and
electricity for her party tomorrow, and what are you gonna
do about that?

CHRIS   Just. Hang on a sec. Hand me that flashlight. I'll
check the circuit breakers.

AMBER *hands him the flashlight.*

AMBER   Don't matter about the circuit breakers if you
ain't paid the minimum, Chris.

CHRIS *exits into the garage.*

AMBER (cont'd)   And now I got wet clothes in the
washer, shit.

AMBER *searches for candles. She doesn't find any, but then she
remembers Janie's birthday candles.*

She opens the pack of candles and lights one.

It doesn't do much. She sticks it in her macaroni.

CHRIS*'s phone chimes on the counter.*

AMBER *looks over at it.*

A beat.

She gets up and checks the phone.

A beat.

CHRIS (off)   It ain't working, Amber.

AMBER *quickly puts the cell phone back on the counter.*

The flashlight shines in the door, and then CHRIS *enters. He's holding a plastic camping lantern.*

AMBER *sits down at the table.*

CHRIS (cont'd)   We got batteries for this?

AMBER   I dunno.

CHRIS   Haven't used it since I went camping with Jim that one time.

AMBER   Yeah, I dunno.

CHRIS *opens drawers, shining the flashlight into them.*

CHRIS   Here's one—maybe that's all it needs.

He opens the lantern, replaces one of the batteries.

The lantern turns on.

CHRIS (cont'd)   Hot damn, look at that.

He sets it on the table.

A beat.

CHRIS (cont'd)   Look, I'm sorry. I fucked up.

AMBER   All the food in the fridge is gonna go bad.

CHRIS   Ah shit.

AMBER   All of it—you know how much I spent on groceries today? There's the chicken, the lunchmeat, the milk for the kids . . .

CHRIS   I bet you this is just a mistake. I bet you the lights come on again in the middle of the night, scare us shitless.

AMBER   I bet you're wrong.

CHRIS   And if they don't, I'll call 'em in the morning.

AMBER   And I told you, tomorrow's Saturday.

CHRIS   So? Someone's gotta be working. People got problems with their electricity any old time.

AMBER   And they're just gonna say, you know. "We didn't get the minimum, so. And it was due weeks ago, so."

CHRIS   So, I'll call 'em anyway. I'll drive over there and hand them twenty-five dollars cash.

AMBER   You don't got twenty-five dollars cash. And it's gonna be hot as shit tonight.

CHRIS   We can open the windows.

AMBER   And how're we gonna have twenty kids running around the house tomorrow? Like having a birthday party inside of an oven.

CHRIS   We can have the party outside.

AMBER   How we gonna do that?

CHRIS   I'll ask Jeff and Betsy if we can use the yard.

AMBER   Janie wants to watch a movie. I asked one of her friend's mom to lend us a DVD player.

CHRIS   We'll get the sprinklers going. Kids like sprinklers.

AMBER   And Jeff and Betsy hate me.

CHRIS   Nah, they don't.

AMBER   Yeah, they do.

CHRIS   Well. They like me, so.

AMBER   This party is gonna be terrible.

CHRIS   No it ain't. Janie's gonna love it. Inside or out.

AMBER   And we don't got no food to feed anyone.

CHRIS   We can ask people to bring food.

AMBER   Oh, that's real classy.

CHRIS   Nah, like a potluck. Oh and—you know what I did today?

AMBER   What did you do today.

CHRIS   I bought one of them big-ass bows for the bicycle. So when we wheel it out tomorrow, it's like. You know. Looks like a present and not just like a bicycle.

AMBER   Yeah.

CHRIS   Like make a big deal of it.

AMBER   Yeah, that'll look great.

CHRIS   Gonna have to teach that girl how to ride a bicycle now.

AMBER   She's been on a bicycle before.

CHRIS   Well, she ain't been on her own bicycle before.

AMBER   We gotta get a helmet before she can go out in the street.

CHRIS   Someone's gotta have one lying around. Little girl's helmet?

AMBER   I guess so.

CHRIS   I didn't wear a helmet when I was growing up.

AMBER   Well. Nowadays you gotta.

CHRIS   I know, I'm just sayin'.
(beat)
You gonna make a wish on that macaroni?

AMBER   No. Just.

She blows out the candle. She eats some of the macaroni, while he picks up the rest of the balloons.

His phone chimes again. He checks it, stuffs it in his pocket.

AMBER *watches him.*

A beat.

CHRIS *sits down at the table with her. He takes a piece of broccoli. He turns down the light on the lantern.*

CHRIS   Kinda romantic.

AMBER   *("Nope")*
Yeah. Kinda.

CHRIS   You know what I'll do?

AMBER   What?

CHRIS   I'll ask Jim if we can put the chicken and the potato salad and all the rest of it in his fridge. Just for the time being. For the party.

AMBER   It's a lot of food.

CHRIS   Well, Jim's got nothing in his fridge, so.

AMBER   You think he's still awake?

CHRIS   I got a key to his place. I'll drive over there.

AMBER   Okay.

CHRIS *opens the fridge, starts pulling stuff out.*

AMBER *gets up to help him.*

CHRIS   Milk, chicken, potato salad . . .

AMBER   Leave the juice. Juice doesn't go bad.

CHRIS   Eggs?

AMBER   Eggs go bad.

CHRIS   Okay.

AMBER   We can leave the birthday cake.

CHRIS   You sure?

AMBER   I think so.

CHRIS   What about the freezer?

AMBER   Ah, shit. I forgot about the freezer.

CHRIS   What do you think?

AMBER *opens the freezer.*

A beat.

AMBER   Bring the popsicles and the chicken nuggets.
Leave the waffles, and the ice is just gonna melt.

They finish packing up the grocery bags.

CHRIS *picks them up and heads toward the garage.*

CHRIS   Can you get the door?

AMBER *does.*

CHRIS *exits.*

AMBER *opens the windows.*

Scene Five

Saturday. Late morning.

A pile of presents is stacked on a kitchen chair. The bicycle is leaning against the table.

AMBER *is making peanut butter and jelly sandwiches at the table.*

LAURA *sits next to her, trying to untangle yards of Christmas tree lights.*

LAURA   It's hot as hell in here.

AMBER   Yeah, well, we can't turn the AC on, so.

A beat.

LAURA   You gonna ask me for money?

AMBER   No and you don't got any money, Mom.

LAURA   I got some savings.

AMBER   I can figure it out.

LAURA   You call 'em?

AMBER   Yeah, I called 'em. Got some customer service whoever-it-was.

LAURA   And what did they say to you about it?

AMBER   They said I paid the minimum for last month but we didn't pay the minimum for this month, and now they won't roll over the balance.

LAURA   Well, what's that mean?

AMBER   It means Chris forgot to pay the minimum this month, and now they ain't turning the electricity back on 'til we can pay off last month's bill in full, even though that ain't what they been doing for years. Chris said he was gonna call 'em too and, I dunno. See if he can get a different answer out of 'em.

LAURA   Huh.
    (beat)
    Then what am I untangling these damn lights for?

AMBER   I dunno, Mom, I told you to stop that.

LAURA   Well. Oh, well.

LAURA *keeps untangling the lights.*

AMBER   And so it's hot as hell in here and it's gonna be hot as hell in here until we pay off the bill.
    (re: the sandwiches)
    How many you think I gotta make?

LAURA   Well. How many kids there gonna be?

AMBER   Let's see. I had to invite everyone in Janie's class so that's twenty-two, but I think only fourteen of 'em said they were gonna come. And there's Max and Sammy. And a couple parents gonna bring their other kids.

LAURA   You ain't giving peanut butter and jelly triangles to the parents, are you?

AMBER   No, Chris is gonna barbecue some chicken on the grill. And the kids can eat that if they want to. And then we got chips and queso and potato salad. And there's gonna be candy in the piñata.

LAURA   Why don't you just use the whole loaf of bread. If they don't get eaten, you can put 'em in the kids lunches next week.

AMBER   They ain't gonna like that.

LAURA   Well, then you tell 'em they can just go hungry they don't want to eat a day-old peanut butter and jelly sandwich. Spoil 'em.

AMBER   All right, Mom.

CHRIS *enters from the living room.*

CHRIS   Hey, Ma, I didn't know you were here already.

He comes over and gives her a kiss on the cheek.

LAURA   Well, everything here got left to the last minute.

CHRIS   Nah, she's done a good job. Amber, you need the car the rest of the day?

AMBER   I got work at the clinic tonight, but not 'til then.

CHRIS   When's that?

AMBER   Like eight?

CHRIS   Shoot.

AMBER   Why?

CHRIS   I just got called in, but I'll get Jim to give me a ride.

AMBER   Called in for the afternoon?

CHRIS   Yeah, they need me there in like. Twenty minutes ago, really.

AMBER   You gonna work the night too?

CHRIS   I dunno. Probably not.

AMBER   So you're gonna miss the party and you ain't even getting the good shift?

CHRIS   What do you want me to tell you?

AMBER   You can't switch with someone?

CHRIS   Ain't no one to switch with. Plus, I tell 'em no, and they won't call me next time.

AMBER   Yeah, I know.

CHRIS   They won't call me in again, you know how it is.

AMBER   Yeah, I know how it is.
   (beat)
   You tell Janie yet?

CHRIS   Not yet.

AMBER   You want me to?

CHRIS   Nah, I'll tell her. And I'll pick her up something special on my way home.

AMBER   Jim still working on the bedroom?

CHRIS   Yeah, he's almost done. I told him we'd just keep the door shut and clean up later.

AMBER   All right.

CHRIS   Hot as shit in there too.

AMBER   Hot as shit everywhere.

CHRIS   Y'all seen the backyard yet?

AMBER   No, how's it look?

CHRIS   Looks real good. Kids are out there taping balloons now. I gotta catch a shower real quick.

He goes.

A beat.

AMBER   Maybe we should grill up some hamburgers too.

LAURA   How much chicken you get?

AMBER   No, just like. In case no one wants the chicken.

LAURA   Well, I can't make heads or tails of these lights. Like they got tangled up in hell.

AMBER   We can't even use them, Mom.

LAURA   I know that. You want me to shove 'em back in
the box all tangled up?

AMBER   I don't care what you do with 'em.

LAURA   Well then.

AMBER *gets up, looks out the window at the kids.*

She bangs on the glass.

AMBER   Max! MAX. Put that stick down right now, you
hear me?

A beat.

LAURA   Birthday parties wasn't such a big thing when
you were a kid.

AMBER   Well. All right.

LAURA   I remember once I took you and your brother
to the movies on your birthday and that was a big treat.
What did we see?

AMBER   *The Little Mermaid.*

LAURA   That's right. Got you anything you wanted from
the candy counter and you drank so much Dr. Pepper I
had to take you out to pee three times during the movie.

AMBER   I loved that movie.

LAURA   What you saw of it.

AMBER   Okay, I think that's it on the bread.

AMBER *puts the peanut butter and jelly jars away. Cleans up a bit around the table.*

AMBER (cont'd)   Mom?

LAURA   Mm?

AMBER   When you were still with Dad, did he ever cheat on you?

A beat.

LAURA   Well, I don't know for sure. I reckon I had, ah. Suspicions.

AMBER   Was that why he left?

LAURA   I dunno. We weren't no good together.

AMBER   Would you have left him? If you knew he was cheating on you? Like for sure?

LAURA   Why you asking me about all this?

AMBER   No reason.

A beat.

LAURA   All I know is I seen Chris running around here all day long fixing up this house for a birthday party for a girl ain't even his own daughter. Fixing up her bedroom. Going off to work a job the rest of the day. That's what I see. I dunno what you see.

AMBER   It's not like. I dunno, Mom. It's not like it's just suddenly easier with him here. I'm the one got two jobs, and he's still another mouth to feed. Another person in the bathroom in the morning. And in and out of work. Can't send a check when he says he gonna send a check. And sometimes he picks up the kids, and sometimes he don't pick up the kids and. And actually? It's easier when I don't gotta think about him. Simpler. Do it on my own. At least I know what gets done and what doesn't get done and I don't have to. I dunno. Think about all the rest of it goes along with him all the time.

LAURA   Well.

AMBER   So.

LAURA   I just don't think that's true.

AMBER   Well, think what you like.

LAURA   Then what're you asking me about it for?

AMBER   I don't know, Mom. Forget it.
(beat)
This is too many sandwiches.

LAURA   And you ain't cutting the crusts off? I remember when Janie wouldn't eat nothing with the crusts.

AMBER   Nah. Some kids like the crust. And if they don't like it, they don't gotta eat it.

LAURA   Ain't no kids like the crust.

AMBER   Well, if we meet the first kid likes the crust today, then he can eat the crust.

LAURA   You got a big Tupperware for these?

AMBER   Yeah, in the . . . over the stove.

A beat.

When LAURA *doesn't get the Tupperware,* AMBER *goes and gets it herself. She puts the sandwiches in it.*

LAURA   I dunno what we did before peanut butter and jelly.

AMBER   Maybe kids weren't as picky before peanut butter and jelly.

LAURA   Amber, I don't think those all gonna fit.

AMBER   Then we'll just have to leave some out, Mom.

JIM *enters from the living room. He's got plaster and dust all over him.*

AMBER (cont'd)   You did not just walk through the living room like that.

JIM   Like what?

AMBER   You're getting dust and shit all over the kitchen. No, just stay there. Take off your boots first.

JIM *unlaces his boots and takes them off. Holds them awkwardly.*

AMBER (cont'd)   You want a towel or something?

JIM   Nah, I'm getting outta here in a minute. Driving Chris down to JJ's, so.

AMBER   Right.

JIM   Just wanted to tell you it's all finished up. Need to paint, but.

AMBER   Oh. Great.

JIM   Yeah, so.

A beat.

AMBER   You thirsty? You want a drink or something?

JIM   Nah, I'm all right.

AMBER   Chris got Miller Lite in a cooler out back. Only cold thing we got in this house.

JIM   That's all right.

AMBER   Well. Suit yourself.

LAURA   You coming to the party, Jim?

JIM   Ah, yes ma'am.

LAURA   Mm.

JIM   Gonna bring back the chicken and the potato salad y'all put in my fridge.

AMBER   Shoot, I was gonna ask Chris to pick up ice cream.

LAURA   There ain't ice cream for the birthday cake?

JIM   Well, I bought a couple gallons for the kids yesterday, you want me to bring it.

AMBER   You didn't have to do that.

JIM   Well. What's cake without ice cream?

AMBER   Well, that'd be great. And if you can bring all the ice you got. And—I think we got an old cooler in the garage somewhere, let me go look for it.

AMBER *exits*.

Beat.

LAURA   Seems like you're the one driving everyone around these days.

JIM   Ain't a big deal.

LAURA   Sure is, gas prices like they are.

JIM   They ain't so bad these days.

LAURA   Is that right?

JIM   Yeah, I dunno.

LAURA   Well.

AMBER *returns with a large cooler.*

AMBER   I guess put the ice cream and the ice in here. The chicken's gonna get grilled anyway. And the potato salad can go in the cooler if there's room for it.

LAURA   Potato salad can sit out.

AMBER   No, it can't, Mom. There's mayonnaise in it.

LAURA   So what?

AMBER   So mayonnaise goes bad in the sun.

LAURA   Oh, you're crazy.

AMBER   I ain't crazy, I just don't want twenty kids going home with food poisoning. That ain't a good party favor.

JIM   It'll fit in there. It ain't that much ice cream.

LAURA   Well, suit yourself.

From the other room:

CHRIS (off)   Jim, you ready to go?

CHRIS *enters in clean clothes.*

JIM   Whenever you are.

AMBER   Chris, you know what time you're gonna be back home?

CHRIS   Ten unless they need me for the late shift too. Look, I gotta go.

AMBER   Kids are still out back.

CHRIS   Right.

CHRIS *goes into the backyard.*

AMBER   Mom, can you stay here 'til Chris gets home? I gotta get to work at eight, so.

LAURA   Hot in this house.

AMBER   Or can you take 'em to your place tonight? Chris can pick 'em up, or. Or they can sleep on the fold-out.

LAURA   I guess that's all right. But I don't got nothing to feed 'em besides my Lean Cuisines.

AMBER   There'll be leftovers from the party.

LAURA   Well, then I guess that's okay.

AMBER   Okay, great.

CHRIS *returns.*

CHRIS   All right, let's do it.

AMBER   You call the electric?

CHRIS   Ah, shoot I forgot. I'll call 'em on the road.

AMBER   Nah, I'll just do it later. Again.

CHRIS   I'll do it. It ain't a problem.

AMBER   Get outta here, you're already late.

CHRIS *gives her a quick kiss.*

CHRIS   Bye, Ma.

LAURA   Bye, Chris.

JIM   Ma'am.

LAURA   Goodbye, Jim.

JIM *takes the cooler, and they go.*

A beat.

LAURA (cont'd)   What else.

AMBER   I dunno. Maybe I should set out some board games. For the kids.

LAURA   You're gonna lose all the pieces in the grass.

AMBER   Then like. Twister or something. We got Twister.

LAURA   Just let 'em run around. Kids can amuse themselves.

AMBER   They need something. Since there ain't a clown now.

LAURA   Well. Maybe Twister, then.

AMBER   It was nice of Jim to pick up that ice cream.

LAURA   Yep.

AMBER   Chris was gonna do that, but.

LAURA   Chris is doing a lot around here.

AMBER   Yeah, Mom, I get it.

(beat)
Do you not like him or something? Jim?

LAURA   Now why would you say that?

AMBER   I just. No reason. Forget it.

LAURA   I barely know the man.

AMBER   You're right. Shoot, now I gotta clean the floors, too. Look like we live in a house full of dirt.

LAURA   Kids are gonna track in dirt from outside anyway.

AMBER   Yeah, but look. There's dust and plaster everywhere. Jesus.

AMBER *gets rags and a bucket from under the sink.*

LAURA   Kids don't notice a little dust.

AMBER   No, but their parents do.

LAURA   Well.

AMBER   Clean the floor. Make the Kool-Aid. Set up the Twister. What else.

A beat.

LAURA   At least it ain't raining.

AMBER   It hasn't rained for six weeks, Mom.

LAURA   Well. At least there's that.

AMBER   Yeah, at least there's that.

A beat.

AMBER *starts to clean the floor.*

LAURA *puts a couple more sandwiches in the Tupperware, then sits back, idly fanning herself.*

LAURA   Christ Almighty, it is hot in here.

AMBER *says nothing, finishes cleaning the floor.*

Scene Six

A few hours later.

The party is going on in full swing in the backyard just outside: sounds of children screaming and laughing and adults chatting can be heard through the open kitchen windows.

AMBER *is alone, leaning on the counter, the cake box in front of her. She is upset about something.*

She takes a moment for herself. The moment is ten seconds long.

Then she snaps herself out of it.

She takes the cake box from the counter and carries it to the kitchen table.

She opens the box and looks at the smushed cake.

A fresh wave of sadness and frustration passes over her.

A beat.

JIM *enters. He watches her for a moment.*

She feels him watching her and looks up.

AMBER   I'll be right out. Just. Getting the cake and the candles and everything.

JIM   You all right?

AMBER   Yeah, Jim, I'm fine.

JIM *doesn't go.*

AMBER (cont'd)   I'm serious. I'm all right. Just.

JIM   She didn't mean it like that. She's out there now riding around on it.

AMBER   Spoiled brat.

JIM   Well. Kids say shit sometimes.

AMBER   "Pink! Gross, Mom!"

JIM   She don't seem to care about none of that no more.

AMBER   And now I'm gonna bring out this smushed-up cake.

JIM   Eh, it ain't so bad.

AMBER   See what she says about that. Ruined.

JIM   Ain't ruined. Bet it tastes just fine.

AMBER   Yeah, well.

JIM   Let me see this.

He goes over to the cake, then gets a butter knife from a drawer.

JIM (cont'd)   Just gotta—

AMBER   See, it's all—

JIM   Eh, eh, eh. Hang on.

He fixes up a corner a bit with the knife.

AMBER *watches.*

JIM (cont'd)   Spread the icing around like that . . .
   (beat)
   You got candles?

AMBER   'Course I got candles.

She gestures to the candles on the counter. JIM *takes out a few candles.*

JIM   Well, all right. So if you put the candles, like. Right here . . . and here . . . like this . . .

He puts the candles on the cake. Counts them. Eight.

JIM (cont'd)   There. Don't look so bad.

AMBER   Still ain't perfect.

JIM   Well. It ain't bad, so.

A beat.

AMBER   Why you doing all this for me?

JIM   Just.

AMBER   You don't even like me.

JIM   Nah.

AMBER   You feel sorry for me or something? 'Cause I
know you ain't doing all this—helping out with all this the
whole day long—'cause you like me, 'cause I know you
don't.

JIM   Nah, that ain't even true.

AMBER   Well. It is true. 'Cause when Chris and I ain't
together, you don't give me the time of day.

JIM   I dunno about that.

AMBER   Tsst. Any time I went round to drop off the
boys—before, when I went round to drop off the boys
with Chris, you barely threw a look at me.

JIM   Well.

AMBER   Yeah, so. So now we're back together and you
gotta be nice to me I guess, so. But I know what you really
think 'cause it's a whole other story when Chris and me
ain't together.

JIM   It ain't true, but. What do you care about what I
think?

AMBER   I don't. I just. Whatever.

JIM   Well. I think Chris is real lucky he got you back this
time. And that's what I told him, so.

A beat.

AMBER   You know anything about this Michelle he's
been texting with?

JIM   I dunno, Amber.

AMBER   Works at JJ's with him? Yeah, I'm sure you don't know nothing about all that. I'm not supposed to know nothing about all that.

JIM   Well.

AMBER   Tsst. You think I'm an idiot.

JIM   I don't think that. But you know how he is, so.

AMBER   Yeah, I know how he is.

JIM   So what do you want me to say about it?

AMBER   You know what? Nothing. I actually don't want you to say nothing about it. And you know what else? And this real sad, Jim. But I figured out the other day that I don't really give two shits if he's sleeping around again. I feel like I'm supposed to, but. I just kinda don't. And I'm like. Surprised that I don't.

JIM   Well, then there ain't no problem.

AMBER   And I don't even know if that's what's actually happening, and you know, I don't even want to know. He can go out there and do that and get caught or not get caught and that's just the way it is.

JIM   All right, then.

AMBER   But you know if I ever went and did something like that. Anything like that. I mean, there ain't no way anyway. Like I got the time or the energy for it if I wanted to. But if I done something like that, I would get just about raked over the fire, over the—whatever that saying is. 'Cause, nuh uh. It doesn't go two ways. And you know Chris would be outta here like that if he found out, and oh, yeah, Jim you can look at me all judgmental and shit about it, but I just don't care. I don't care about any of it. Whatever he does.

JIM   Then it seems like you got it all worked out.

AMBER   But it ain't fair. Ain't fair that he's gonna go through his life being the same guy he always is, same guy he always was, but I gotta go through my life like. Like I gotta lose just about everything I used to like about myself just so I can keep shit even halfway decent for everyone else around here.

A beat.

JIM   I dunno what you mean about that.

AMBER   Just. I been with Chris since before I was even a grown-up person. And I ain't the same person, and that's how it goes. But I miss that person I used to be. You know?

JIM   I guess so.

AMBER   All right. Whatever, Jim.

JIM   Look, you're married to my brother. So, what do you want me to say?

AMBER   Nothing. You don't gotta say nothing. It's— whatever.

A beat.

JIM   So you remember when you and Chris started dating?

AMBER   Yeah, Jim. I remember.

JIM   I know you two was on and off for a long while, but. But like when you just started seeing each other for the first time, you remember that?

AMBER   Yeah, I remember that. So what?

JIM   So I dunno. You know what I think about sometimes?

AMBER   What's that?

JIM   I dunno, it ain't special or nothin' like that. You and Chris were still in high school, and I was a few years outta high school. More'n a few years outta high school. And, ah. And one day—you remember Chris's car back then? Piece of shit Corolla or whatever it was? It gave out one day and I told him I'd give you and him a ride back to our house after school, or I guess I wasn't still living there but Chris was and, ah. Well, you remember. So we were all hanging out that day. Watching the TV or. I dunno what.
   And I went out on the porch to have a cigarette 'cause Ma didn't like it when we smoked in the house, and I was sitting there smoking on the porch and not thinking about anything in particular. And you came out after me and you asked me if you could bum a cigarette, and I gave you one and I lit it for you and we were smoking for a second and not saying anything to each other. Just sorta. Sitting there on the porch looking out at the other houses in the neighborhood. Cars passing by every once in a while. That asshole dog the neighbors had next door that barked all the goddamned time.

And you and me didn't ever really talk a lot, and I guess we don't talk a lot now either, like still or whatever. And we were sitting out there smoking for a second, like. I dunno, like I guess how we used to do. And, ah. And that day it was real hot and muggy, but I guess it wasn't all that bad 'cause it was September. And you had those bangs back then you had to flick out of your eyes all the time and you were wearing this old Dallas Cowboys t-shirt I think it used to belong to Chris and a pair of cutoff jean shorts.

And, ah. Anyway. We were sitting there for a little bit and then you sorta turned and half looked at me and you said, "So. What's your story, Jim?" sorta like you were teasing me but also sorta like you weren't. And it made me laugh 'cause no one'd ever said that to me before, like that.

And I don't remember what I said to answer that, probably just sorta. Shrugged it off, but I guess that ain't really important. And, ah. Then I said to you, like back at you, "So. What's your story, Amber?" And you take a drag of your cigarette and you give me this look like. I dunno. Like we're old pals already. And you say, "Well. That is a long story, Jim." And you sorta smile at me and I sorta smile back and. I felt like I knew exactly what you meant. Like I could see that long story rolling around inside your head, and you didn't have to say nothing more about it. And I know that's the kinda thing some people just say, sorta like a joke, and maybe that's how you meant it, but I also know it was true when you said, and.

And then we sat there and finished our cigarettes and, ah. What'd we do next. Guess we went back inside the house. Hung around with Chris. Watched the TV. Played with the dogs. Made some food or Ma brought home Whataburger. Nothing special. Anyway.

I think about that sometimes. I think about sitting on the porch with you that afternoon and. And talking to you like that. And you talking to me like that. And how it felt to me like I was getting this entire person, easy as that. Like I still do, I reckon. Like I was getting all of you in the time it took to smoke a cigarette on the porch. Like we were gonna do a hundred times after that and. I dunno. Well.

A long beat.

A lot happens in this beat for AMBER.

Then:

AMBER   The cake. I should—

JIM   Yeah, go ahead. You need a light?

AMBER   Nah, I got one.

AMBER *picks up the cake. She starts to head outside with it. She stops.*

AMBER (cont'd)   Thank you. Ah. It really looks a lot better now.

JIM   No big deal.

AMBER   Well.

JIM   Well.

AMBER   You want a piece, you better get out there quick. These kids can put away a cake like you would not believe.

JIM   All right, I will.

AMBER *goes.*

JIM *stays in the kitchen for a minute.*

Scene Seven

Late at night.

The lights are still out, but AMBER *has lit candles and the lantern sits in the center of the kitchen table.*

AMBER *enters with a bag of trash and carries it out the back door.*

She returns and starts washing the stack of dishes in the sink.

A beat.

CHRIS *enters, exhausted from a ten-hour shift at JJ's.*

CHRIS
    (re: the candles)
    What's all this?

AMBER   What do you mean? Lights are still out, so.

CHRIS   And what're you doing here?

AMBER   I got cut. Linda scheduled three of us, but they only ever want two.

CHRIS   That sucks.

AMBER   Yup. That's eighty bucks we ain't seeing next week.

CHRIS   Well, I made ninety-five, so we're seeing that.

AMBER   And I'm always the one that gets cut. Always.
Because I won't kiss her fat ass like the rest of 'em do.

CHRIS   Hey, why don't you give the cleaning up a break.
Go lay down on the bed for a sec. For the whole night.

AMBER   'Cause if I leave this mess here all night we'll
get roaches again and I don't want to deal with that. So I
gotta clean all this shit tonight. And there's leftovers
gonna go bad and I got coolers and no ice and Tupperware I gotta wash out and give back to the people lent 'em
to me. And there's balloons everywhere. All over the
backyard. Little like. Balloon pieces everywhere.

CHRIS   I'll pick up the balloons.

AMBER   Not just balloons. Balloon pieces. Everywhere.

CHRIS   I'll get 'em all up in the morning. Every single
balloon piece.

AMBER   And I told you there's gonna be balloons
everywhere. Kids popping 'em all day long. And you
can't just get 'em all up in the morning, they're in the
trees and little pieces on the roof. We ain't never gonna
get rid of 'em.

CHRIS   First time it rains, it's gonna. You know. Flush
'em out.

AMBER   And when's that gonna be?

CHRIS   But I'll get 'em all up anyway.

AMBER   Hot as shit in here too, and there's cigarette butts all over the yard like no one ever heard of an ashtray.

CHRIS   Then I'll pick those up too.

AMBER   Or a plastic cup with an inch of water in it.

CHRIS   Something happen today?

AMBER   What does that mean.

CHRIS   You're in worse a mood than usual tonight.

AMBER   Same old shit.
   (beat)
   It's just been a long day.

CHRIS   Okay.
   (beat)
   So how was it?

AMBER   How was what?

CHRIS   The party.

AMBER   Good. Fine.

CHRIS   What'd Janie say about the bicycle?

AMBER   She loved it. Practically glued to the seat, riding it around all afternoon.

CHRIS   I'll get her a helmet at Walmart tomorrow.

AMBER   Okay.

CHRIS   What time you got work?

AMBER   10:30 unless they call me in earlier.

CHRIS   Okay, I'll drop you off and then I'll get the kids up from your ma's after that. Take 'em all to Walmart. We need anything else?

AMBER   I don't think so.

CHRIS   Okay.

A beat.

AMBER   How was JJ's?

CHRIS   Just the same old shit.

AMBER   You got home quick tonight.

CHRIS   Yeah, Pat does Saturday nights. Makes a shit-ton of money, too.

AMBER   Well.

CHRIS   Ninety-five ain't so bad though. Better'n the afternoon shift during the week.

AMBER   So you got a ride home?

CHRIS   Yup.

AMBER   Who gave it to you?

CHRIS   One of the barbacks.

AMBER   Okay.

CHRIS   Guy named Emilio.

AMBER   Okay.

A beat.

CHRIS   Hey, so it was a good party, then?

AMBER   I guess so.

CHRIS   Got any of that cake left?

AMBER   Not a crumb of it.

CHRIS   Ah, shoot. I been dreaming about that cake all day long.

AMBER   Oh yeah?

CHRIS   Maybe I'll pick up another birthday cake tomorrow when we head over to the Walmart.

AMBER   Well, don't drop this one on the floor, that's my advice to you.

CHRIS   You said something about leftovers?

AMBER   Couple pieces of chicken and a lot of potato salad, but I dunno, I might just have to throw it out. Sitting in the sun all day long.

CHRIS   Hey, you know what I just realized?

AMBER   What's that?

CHRIS   We got the whole house to ourselves all night long.

AMBER   Is that right?

CHRIS   Looks like it to me. Unless you got someone else over here tonight.

AMBER   Oh, yeah, my boyfriend is coming over in like an hour if you could make yourself scarce.

CHRIS   Oh, really?

AMBER   Mmhm.

CHRIS   That's why all the candles, then.

AMBER   Oh, yeah, he likes it real romantic.

CHRIS   Well, I think I'd like to meet him.

AMBER   Yeah, I think the two of you will be great friends.

CHRIS   Come over here.

AMBER   Hang on, my hands are all wet.

CHRIS   I don't care, come over here.

She doesn't, so he gets up, goes to her, and pulls her to him.

They kiss. It's pretty hot.

CHRIS (cont'd)   I don't get you all to myself that much.

AMBER   Well, what do you expect?

CHRIS   I don't expect. It's just nice, that's all.

And it is nice.

AMBER   You remember when we were just kids?

CHRIS   Sure.

AMBER   You remember that time we were laying in the back of that pickup truck? I think it was Mallory's, but I forget.

CHRIS   What about it?

AMBER   You said, "Amber Larson, I'm gonna marry you." Just like that. You remember that?

CHRIS   Well, and I did, didn't I?

AMBER   Yeah, but do you remember that night? You remember that pickup truck?

CHRIS   There was a lot of nights like that.

AMBER   I guess so.

CHRIS   I remember I was crazy about you. Still am crazy about you. Like I'm always gonna be.

He kisses her, real gently this time.

They stand there, together in the kitchen, for a moment.

AMBER   Hey.

And CHRIS *kisses her again, and this is a real kiss, a something is going to happen kiss.*

AMBER *kisses him back.*

Then she pulls away from him before things go farther.

AMBER (cont'd)   Nah, go on to the bedroom.

CHRIS   What's the matter?

AMBER   Nothing, I'll be there in a sec.

CHRIS *isn't convinced.*

AMBER (cont'd)   Let me finish up some of this shit out here, otherwise it'll be bothering me all night.

CHRIS   All right. Sure I can't help?

AMBER   Nah, you are bone-tired, even I can see that. Go lay down or catch a shower or whatever you want to do. I'll be in there in a second.

She pulls him into her, kisses him deeply, and then pushes him away.

AMBER (cont'd)   Go on, then.

CHRIS   All right. But don't you take too long. Otherwise I'ma come back here and you are gonna be in real trouble.

AMBER   Is that right?

CHRIS   You bet it is.

AMBER   All right.

He goes.

AMBER (cont'd)   Will you make sure the windows are open in the bedroom?

CHRIS (off)   Yes, ma'am.

AMBER   It's hot as shit in there.

A beat.

She starts to pick up around the kitchen again.

She hears the shower running offstage.

She gets a pack of cigarettes from on top of the refrigerator.

She sits at the table in silence and smokes an entire cigarette.

This is AMBER*'s monologue, and it is wordless.*

This moment must last no less than two and a half uninterrupted minutes. It can be held for up to four minutes.

Suddenly, after this long, long beat, the lights come on.

AMBER *takes in this miracle for a moment.*

CHRIS (off)   Holy shit! You see that out there?

AMBER   Yeah! Yeah, turn on the AC when you get out of the shower!

CHRIS (off)   What?

AMBER   The AC!

CHRIS (off)   What?

AMBER   Never mind!

AMBER *goes to the bedroom, turns on the AC, closes all the windows.*

She comes back, blows out the candles, turns off the lantern, and closes the windows in the kitchen.

Then she sits at the kitchen table and she does absolutely nothing for about ten glorious seconds.

She hears the shower turn off, and she gets up from the table and heads toward the bedroom to join CHRIS.

END OF PLAY